# hello, I'm
# EMBARRASSMENT

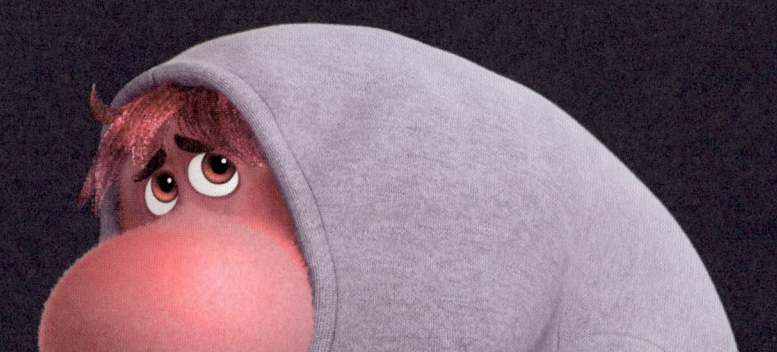

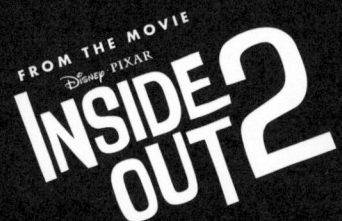

# hello, I'm EMBARRASSMENT

**Editor** Emma Wolf
**Art Editor** Rick DeLucco
**Managing Editor** Hazel Eriksson
**Senior Production Editor** Jennifer Murray
**Senior Production Controller** Louise Daly
**Jacket Designer** Rick DeLucco
**Jacket Editor** Emma Wolf
**Publisher** Jelani Memory
**Managing Director** Mark Searle

First published in Great Britain in 2025 by
Dorling Kindersley Limited
20 Vauxhall Bridge Road,
London SW1V 2SA
A Penguin Random House Company

The authorised representative in the EEA is
Dorling Kindersley Verlag GmbH. Arnulfstr. 124, 80636 Munich, Germany

Page design copyright © 2025 Dorling Kindersley Limited
10 9 8 7 6 5 4 3 2 1
001–355980–Oct/2025

Copyright © 2025 Disney Enterprises, Inc. and Pixar. All rights reserved.

Without limiting the rights under the copyright reserved above,
no part of this publication may be reproduced, stored in or introduced into a retrieval system, or transmitted, in any form, or by any means (electronic, mechanical, photocopying, recording, or otherwise), without the prior written permission of the copyright owner. DK values and supports copyright. Thank you for respecting intellectual property laws by not reproducing, scanning or distributing any part of this publication by any means without permission. By purchasing an authorised edition, you are supporting writers and artists and enabling DK to continue to publish books that inform and inspire readers.
No part of this publication may be used or reproduced in any manner for the purpose of training artificial intelligence technologies or systems. In accordance with Article 4(3) of the DSM Directive 2019/790, DK expressly reserves this work from the text and data mining exception.

A CIP catalogue record for this book is available from the British Library.
ISBN 978-0-2417-8874-5

Printed and bound in China

www.dk.com
www.disney.com

Hello, I'm
# EMBARRASSMENT.

# What's that?

You want me to start?
Really?! Honestly,
I'm not very good
at this sort of thing.

I'm not really big on...
well, talking.

When I do,
it makes people
pay attention to me,
which is the one
thing I never want.

**You probably know what it's like to not want attention!**

**RIGHT?** **MAYBE?**

**PROBABLY?** **NO?**

I should probably stop talking, huh?

**Of course not, pal! You're doing great!**

HI THERE! MY NAME IS JOY.

**And I think Embarrassment – while he can be a bit shy – is really doggone great!**

EVERYONE CAN LEARN A THING OR TWO FROM HIM. ISN'T THAT RIGHT, BIG GUY?!

**Embarrassment, buddy, do you want to try to tell folks a little bit about what it feels like to be you?**

I PROMISE YOU'VE GOT THIS!

Well, I'm that feeling you feel...

when you want to disappear.

Well, you *feel* like you want to disappear, but you can't do that in this book.

**TELL THEM SOMETHING ELSE ABOUT YOU!**

Um, well, I am often the last emotion you want to feel.

I'm not like my other friends like ANXIETY, ANGER, JOY, or even SADNESS.

They all seem to just make sense.

But I just make you feel all weird, hot, sad, and shy all at the same time.

I'm sorry about that – I can't seem to help it.

IT'S JUST WHO I AM.

Most of the time
I don't think
I'm good at...

# ANYTHING.

**That all I do is make things worse.**

Hey, Embarrassment. I think you can be really helpful sometimes!

Like when someone says something they thought was really cool and funny, but it actually hurt their friend's feelings.

It's important to feel embarrassed when you do that.

Then you can apologise and make things right again.

RIGHT, EMBARRASSMENT?

I guess you
might be right...

Maybe I'm not as
awful as I thought –

# SORRY, SORRY, SORRY,

I didn't mean to cut you off but I just couldn't help myself! I also think you're pretty helpful!

LIKE WHEN SOMEONE DOESN'T FEEL READY FOR SOMETHING, LIKE A BIG TALENT SHOW, FEELING EMBARRASSED THEN MIGHT JUST MEAN IT'S NOT THE RIGHT TIME.

WHICH IS OK!!

Honestly, you're just really good at keeping people from hurting themselves, or someone else.

# REALLY?
# I AM?
# WOW...
# THANKS.

I guess... if I could explain a bit about what it's like to be me... I'd say it's like maybe you have to get up in front of your class and do a big presentation, and even though you spent all night memorising everything you wanted to say, *now* when you're up in front of everyone you can't seem to get the right words out, your cheeks get all hot and red, and you wish you could hide under your desk and no one would ever look at you again!

**...OR SOMETHING LIKE THAT. AWFUL, RIGHT?**

I know I can
feel awkward,
uncomfortable, and
sometimes no good.

But I don't really know what to do about it except keep being me.

...OK, I feel like I'm doing a lot of talking.

Am I being too much?

YES?! Oh wait, no?

Oh, I thought you said yes, but I guess I can't really hear you because I'm in this book and you're not.

Sorry, this is just what I'm like.

OH, I'M SO EMBARRASSED...

# CLASSIC EMBARRASSMENT!

I LOVE YOU, BUDDY. THAT NEVER GETS OLD.

IS THERE ANYTHING ELSE YOU WANT TO SHARE WITH OUR FRIENDS READING THIS BOOK?

**Well... There *is* something that I'm really proud of...**

REALLY?! THAT IS SO EXCITING. TELL US! TELL US! **TELL US!**

# OK... here it goes...

I know it doesn't feel good to feel embarrassed.

But you can be proud, knowing that when I do show up, it means you're being...

COURAGEOUS,
BRILLIANT,
AND AMAZING!

# WHICH IS SO INCREDIBLY AND AMAZINGLY AWESOME, RIGHT?!

Right?

Oh boy, I did it again, didn't I?

Sorry... sometimes I just can't help myself.

**But I meant what I said! And I'm not embarrassed to say it.**

(WHICH I KNOW IS KIND OF WEIRD BECAUSE I AM EMBARRASSMENT, BUT YEAH.)

**So, what should you do when you feel embarrassed?**

I'm no expert, but I'd start by just closing your eyes.

Taking a breath.

And then taking another...

# REMEMBER — YOU'RE COURAGEOUS.

**And it's OK
to feel however
you feel.**

Even if it's

# EMBAR

RASSED.

# More from the series.

# Discover these conversation starters.

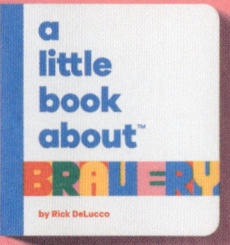 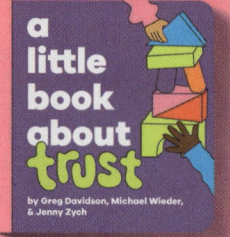 

www.dk.com